Gather the Stars
and Hang the Moon

Gather the Stars
and Hang the Moon

TARA SHANNON

echo
BOOKS

an imprint of
Wintertickle Press

Wintertickle Press
132 Commerce Park Drive
Unit K, Ste. 155
Barrie, ON L4N 0Z7

WintericklePress.com
@WintertcklePress

ISBN 978-1-989664-12-4

For Kid Big and Kid Little

CONTENTS

THE WOMAN WHO WRITES

The woman who writes
has a depth of soul
like an abyss…
Dark and frightful at first glimpse
Many turn away
unwilling to stay
Afraid to thumb the pages of her book
It's written in blood
In tears and fears
and with laughter and love
Its sanguine ink soaks through every page
and its subject matter is sage
Beginning in well-worn memories
that last on forever
far beyond her earthbound years

Learn to love her
this woman who writes
She is worth the effort
because within her lies a labyrinth of scars
encompassed by a wisdom and a love so large
it could only be rivalled by the magnitude and
complexity of a universe full of stars

She is there for you to explore
To have, to hold, to love
Just be patient and be kind

And of course
dare to step inside

DANGEROUS WOMAN

Fear
stripped me bare,
peeling away
every bit of who
and what
I thought I was

Until

I was.

And I wasn't pretty.

My knees trembled
while the ground beneath threatened to give way

I cried
and screamed

from a place within
buried so deep
that at first
the noises I emoted
didn't even sound like me

And don't think I'm now going to say that I simply
picked myself up and carried on,
head held high

Because I didn't

I crumbled beneath the weight of it

My fear
and the ghosts that spun around me echoed out
in the darkness threatening to take everything
away

To which
I replied,
"Go ahead."

There was nothing left for me to lose

"Go ahead!"
I dared.

Still
and silence
followed

Awkwardly
I sat with myself
healing generations old wounds

And that's when it began to change

That's when I changed

When I took back control of the game that had
for so long been trying to play me

I accepted myself

And with that
I knew there wasn't anything

   should I choose

That I could not do.

That's when I became —
A dangerous woman

I AM THE MOON

There's a part of me that doesn't exist anymore
She lays shattered on the ground of my childhood home
waiting for her mother
who left her there
all alone

What was left of me
Limped
Contorted
Through a version of life
that seemed much more a dream
Unreal
Surreal
Blood dripping to the floor
everywhere I went
leaving a trail for the monsters to find me
They lurked around corners
in mundane places both
in dreams
and daylight

I fumbled and fell in the darkness
until one day
light seeped in
I turned away
unused to its ways
But I listened to its whispers

Of hope

It threw open the curtains
and shook off the dust

I had collapsed inward
and still somehow made it through
to the other side
Swept out with the tide
into a limitless ocean
Filled with phosphorus that changed into stars as the
horizon merged with the night sky

I am the moon

Shifting through phases
Sometimes hidden
Sometimes seen

Yet somehow

Always whole

MELANCHOLIA

This is about my journey to find one of my great-grandmothers. She was, I believe, at least in part, at the root of some of the trauma or "things we didn't talk about" on that side of my family.

My great-grandmother was born in rural Ireland in 1863, and I believe her parents converted to protestantism for survival during the Great Famine. Her mother (my great-great-grandmother) died while my great-grandmother was quite young, and life was undoubtedly hard for all of them in many ways. For my great-grandmother, things only seemed to get worse.

Her existence and death became somewhat unknown to subsequent generations, likely because the cause of her death was a taboo subject — that, and her brother who lived next door, completed suicide following his wife's untimely death. It must have been a very scary and sad time for all the family and the residents of the area, compounded by the fact that they likely didn't speak of it. I know they didn't speak of it because no one in my family knew any of this until I uncovered it doing my research.

MELANCHOLIA

It's where I hoped you wouldn't be
but yet
there you are
draped in sadness
the kind that seeps into your bones
like a cool damp
Irish night

no matter what you do
you can't quite shake it...

I've seen it before
when his smile would fade
and ill humour would replace it

When silence

.

.

.

would invade
at an almost intolerable pitch

It found me too
from time to time
I felt it
eating away at my bones
gnawing at my happiness
until it was full, and it would leave

until the next time

It was a monster I didn't understand
lurking in the shadows
while I stood, tripping over eggshells
wondering
Why was it here?
Why did it come...

and choose me...

choose us?

And then, I found you
in that place where I knew you'd be
even though I hoped you wouldn't
after all other avenues had run out of turns

There you were

and I understood
generations of pain

Sarah Kennedy
Mother of seven
Died of Melancholia
Age, 32

SARAH KENNEDY

Miles away, across the ocean on the north-west coast of Ireland, there sits an old forgotten farmhouse whose walls remain strong and steadfast. No amount of wind or rain has been able to break down their defenses. Against the backdrop of the sea and the radiant green of the farms, hills, and fields that surround it, it appears cold and dead. So much life, moving and breathing beyond its walls. On the shores of the beach nearby and visible from the house at almost every turn are grey seals, beginning their annual venture back to dry land. Here, they will mate or, on a quiet beach, give birth to a new generation. They will take up residence for nearly three months so their young can grow strong enough to be left on their own. Their mothers care for them, teaching them and defending them against the world they will soon be part of: The bitter reality of the sea on a cold winter's day and the evil of men who may try to ensnare them. Once ready, mother and pup will part ways. Possibly to meet up again in time on the same beach so the cycle may begin again.

Back on land, cattle and sheep lazily roam the fields. Green tufts of grass and late summer flowers peek out through each little crevice along the garden walls while a fox trots and scurries, feasting on nearby brambles. A raven calls out from the rooftop, telling the story of those who used to live here. Is it a fairytale with an unhappy ending? No human ears are deft enough to tell, and those who need to hear it are far away. But no amount of time or space can prevent the song from reaching its intended. Carrying on the breeze, the song echoes into their ears. A strange and haunting melody pulling them to return.

Deep inside the cold grey stone house, there is a heart that still beats, soft and slow. There's life in the old place yet. It's a little over a hundred and fifty years old and has seen its share of ups and downs, heartache, laughter, songs, and a dance or two. But, it's the violence and the secrets that made her grow cold. Leaving her alone and wanting at the edge of the sea. Longing to live again, the life she was meant to lead.

A strong gust of wind opens the front door and every window is thrown open. A new chance at life is coming. A chance to rewrite old wrongs and to start over.

It's just a matter of time.

Every stone that makes up this farmhouse, sitting perched at the edge of the ocean, it's outbuildings and border walls, were set into place, one by one by a pair of unyielding hands. This is the house that Edward built. He was not alone, though, he would tell you that he was. No, the foundation of this place was deeply rooted not by one man, but by the many who came before him and by those who dwelt thereafter. Those men were quietly held up by the perseverance of the women who lived by their side. When Edward built this place, *she* was here too. However, you won't find her name written down anywhere. Her name has only been whispered through the generations. A ghost lost from the annals of history. Not written down on purpose; his purpose. It didn't suit Edward that she should be named. She was undeserving.

She has only ever been a footnote to his story…until now.

IN A FLASH

And just like that
My skin is hot
Sweat beading at my brow
I hurry to the window
Throwing it open
Breathing a sigh of relief
As cool air breaths reprieve
Over flushed cheeks
No more do they blush
Fresh with youth
Oh no, now they burn hot
With fiery rage
For I am woman!
And heavy is the crown

Or is it crone?

Hear me roar

GOOD GIRL

at an early age I learned
that's what men want
and some women too

a girl who doesn't rock the boat
who does what she's told
with a smile

"Smile"
"You should smile more"
"You're prettier when you smile"
I'd smile, like some kind of automaton
fake, in a fake world

Good girl

I hated it
and a rage began to build inside

Good girl

Good girl

Good girl

Do as you're told

Don't talk back
Smile
Nod

Good girl

His hand rested on my leg

I shoved it away
and said to myself

"Good girl"

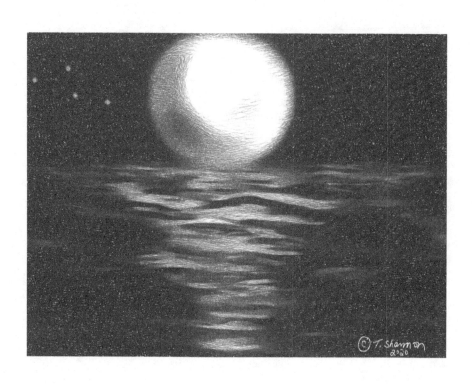

CUNNING

Was it old wives' tales and superstition...or was it
something more...?

Cunning.
That's what they called themselves
   through smoke clouds and whispers
      My mother, her sisters, my grandmother

         and me
            ...hanging. on. every. word...

as we sat round the table
rolling cigarettes
and rolling the dice

And when I grew too tired, I would go to bed
Their laughter and stories following me
up through the vent into my room
long into the night

Yahtzee! Someone would call
Followed by laughter
accusations of cheating...

Then, the serious less excitable talk of the world
and *As the World Turns*
would resume

They knew things...

these women

By the rising and setting of the sun
the phase of the moon
the way of the wind and clouds
and the telltale flickering of the light

Was it magic? I wondered
as I tried to learn their ways

Capturing its essence
and bottling it up
Saving it for a rainy day

It wasn't magic
they'd laugh
then cough
then laugh again

It was a gift that many simply learned
to forget
amidst the quest to tune in and connect
there was a

      disconnect - - -

dead air on the line
No one wanting to be alone

with their own thoughts

To me

it was magic

and that's how I think of it still
when it sometimes comes calling
in the early morning hours

still dressed as night

Break the Cycle

It's a strange thing...
to love someone
and loathe them
   at the same time

But, sometimes that's what abuse looks like

It's a paradox
It's conditioning
It's...
expected

It's
...
control

And it becomes nOrMaL

That's what makes looking back so hard
Reconciling the contradictions
and the false sense of self

Some will say...don't
Don't look back
Only move forward

I say...
Sometimes to move forward
we must look back

Otherwise, some cycles
may never break

EARTH AND SKY

Once upon a time, only the earth and sky existed
One always looking up, and the other forever down
Never to touch
though they wished they could
So, they spent every moment together, chasing the
horizon

and that spot in the distance where it appeared that
the land met the sky
two becoming one
but it was only an illusion
Nevertheless, they followed the path of the fading
sun endlessly
that is, until one day when a star fell, tearing through
the sky with a blazing tail and landing with a thud
into the earth

"Did you feel that?" asked the sky.
"I did, and I do," said the earth.
And, for the first time in millions of years the two
turned away from the fading sun so they could
retrace their steps and discover that which they both
had felt...
It wasn't long before they discovered a great crater
exposing the dirt and rock beneath the earth's
surface
"Does it hurt?" asked the sky.
"No," said the earth. "But I do feel something moving
within."
And the two watched as the first wellspring
gurgled up from the ground

It pushed in, and spilled out across the land in
every direction
nourishing the earth, feeding the soil and
reshaping the rock as it went
Soon, there was a pool of water large enough
for the sky to see itself reflected in the earth
but still the two could not touch
They resumed their chase
Many more years passed until once more, the
earth felt something stirring within
"What is it?" asked the sky.
"I don't know," replied the earth.
Again, the two retraced their steps, this time
meeting the sun as it began to rise. And there,
within the glowing light, they watched a
creature emerge from the soil.
Fed by the nearby wellspring, it grew a little
more with every sip. Stretching deeper into the
earth and higher into the sky until at long last it
took a deep breath
and caressed the clouds

"I felt that," said the sky.
"So did I," said the earth.
And it was then, born of a seed planted in the
earth and nourished by a star that had fallen
from the sky, that the earth and sky touched for
the first time,
united in the birth of the very first tree
all of them connected
water and roots
earth and sky

You are the earth
and I am the sky

DREAMER

"You're a dreamer," you say,
"with your head stuck up in the clouds."

You make it sound like that's a bad thing
And I wonder...
Why is it that you want to bring me down?

There's nothing wrong with dreaming
Dreamers are the magic makers
Making wishes and holding on to hope
Working diligently
Quietly
Long into the night

Yet, you don't even notice that we're here...

Until one day we emerge, wings unfurled
Standing strong
Absorbing your light

"You're a dreamer," you say.

Not knowing who I am
Or where I've been
And all I've seen

You see what you want to see
Cast in the shadow of your own doubt

But that's not me

I am not you

Don't paint me with that brush

Goals are my dreams
Forged in starlight
Humming on the breeze

I am a dreamer.

With my head up in the clouds.

Dreaming of unending possibilities
Nothing impossible
Nothing out of reach

My dreams

Are coming true.

I am a dreamer.

Who are you?

...a star is not a star without having experienced darkness and complete collapse.

FIRE!

My house is on f i r e
So, I do nothing
   but watch

...scrolling my feed
pretending to care
with my likes and my shares

I *add to cart*
It's the latest nonsense
aimed to bring joy

but it doesn't.

I buy more.

It's not until my chair begins

to b u r n
that I think

"Maybe I should do something...?"

but it's too late

And really, I shouldn't have struck the match in the
first place
I mean, I watched my parents do it
and theirs too

What was I supposed to do?

If only I could stop it
If only I knew how

It's just how it is.

My house is on f i r e

and I'm going to watch it b u r n

ONCE UPON A TIME

Fairytales...they're often the first stories many of us hear, read, or watch as children.

We continue to tell them and retell (or reimagine) them to each new generation.

What do they teach us? Well, that's a big question because they can teach us many things. It's the storyteller's spin, of course, that guides the tale, and usually there is a much deeper, sometimes hidden, meaning than may first meet the eye.

Fairytales are old. They're much older than Disney and they span the globe. Every single country or culture on this earth has their own fairytales or folklore. They begin as stories told around the fire as a form of entertainment. Then they evolve based on the storyteller, and where they're being told, or to whom they're being told to. They contain bits of history, customs, news of the day, warnings, a quest, good and evil, light over dark...magic.

Sometimes these stories are forgotten, lost to war, conquest, or emigration. Think Ireland and the British Isles — although, in Ireland, at least early Christian monks were writing some of the old stories down, preserving them, skewed though they may be. At least they exist in some form. Regardless, many Irish (and Scots, Welsh, British, etc.) went out into the world without their stories. And, that's sad indeed—to be out there in the world without our stories.

Our old stories not only link us to who we are or were, but they also connect us to other cultures around the world. At the root many of these core stories (folklore, fairytales, creation stories), there are parallels. And those similarities have the potential to drive empathy and understanding — something we are missing in the world today.

To think that loss of empathy and understanding for others could be tied to a loss of story — that's big. To me, it is anyway. Thankfully, we can do something about it; we can attempt to relearn some of our lost stories through the efforts of scholars and storytellers who are actively researching and sharing what they find. Perhaps in the process, we may find that connection we have been missing to others and to ourselves.

And this is where I want to start. It's where I think each of us must start. With ourselves.

This is something big that many fairytales tell us, the way out — to that *happy ever after* (whatever that may be, for it will look different for each of us).

Through the dark forest...

Through facing and overpowering the evil queen or witch...

Through outsmarting the troll...

Through the defeat of the terrible fire-breathing dragon...

Through confronting the ghost that haunts the house...or your mind...or the monster under the bed, in the closet, in the basement or in the attic...

Through dealing with the troubling thoughts or memories that persist day after day...

Whatever that *darkness* or trauma is that manifests inside almost every one of us — that's what we must face. And not to save the princess — but to save ourselves.

OH CANADA...

It was never their shame
their silence
or their secret

It's ours.

#everychildmatters

I LOVE YOU

I met myself one day
after I'd fallen apart

I lay on the ground
   limbs shattered and torn
      mind tired and weary
         heart
            broken

Everything lost
and nothing left to lose

Surely the ground would swallow me up
I thought
I hoped

But it didn't

The earth from which I came
wouldn't reclaim me
I wondered if I were poison?

I lay there a while longer
eyes closed
the earth breathing beneath me
deep exaggerated breaths

I matched its rhythm

and when I did

My limbs stitched back together
  My mind relaxed
    and my heart began to mend

And...

I saw her

standing there

staring in
and out through my eyes

She reached for me with my mother's hands
smiling a beautiful, storied smile

Myself.

I love you, she said

And I believed her

I Believe

As I sit here, I start thinking

Thinking, thinking
Without blinking

Can Dragons fly?
Of course, they can
Flittering off to Neverland

Butters fly
This I know
They flutter sweetly to and fro

Butters practice pure persistence
Shimmering in
And out of existence
Transforming, shaping, and flying high
Then, so softly, landing by

Dragons too, fly about
Wings humming in and out
Not as dainty as the Butter
Whoso sweetly flits and flutters
Dragons zipper all around

Is it lost
Or is it found?

What of Dragons and of Butters?
Do they dazzle one another?
Here on earth, within my mind, they dazzle me every time

My eyes are open. My book is read
But of them, what can be said?
Can they see me — are they blind?
Are they weary of mankind?

They join together in their chorus
Wafting gently through the forest
Singing softly, by the by
A sweet, silken lullaby

I'm captivated; mesmerized
And if I were to surmise
I do believe they're in disguise
Those fluttering, floating, fleeting flies

These two creatures do bemuse
A quiet question to amuse...
What if fairy tales are true?

I believe
Do you?

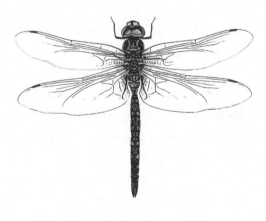

MEDICINE AND MAGIC

Barefoot on fresh cut grass, early in the morning.
The dew glistening like diamonds as far as the eyes
can see.
A symphony of crickets and a cacophony of birds
greet this slow but steady new day.
There's beauty and hope on the warm breeze —
can you feel it?

Can you taste the memories that begin to flow?
Taking you back to a time that,
though now faded by the sun,
was perfect
and timeless;
seemingly endless.

You wish that you could go back.

But you can't.

So, soak it in — the sun, the scent of the grass, the
crickets and the birds and the dew on your feet.

It's medicine and it's magic.
And ever so dreamily you begin to wonder if they
can be bottled and stored?

No, not really...but you can write them down,
these thoughts and feelings and memories that
clamour at the garden gate of your mind

Hurry, though, and capture them
before they're gone.
They're galloping toward the fields at the back of the
house.

Ready to launch and soar away into the
afternoon sky.
Gone again for another day,
when your memories and senses may offer up
something new
and possibly not quite so sweet.

STILL AND QUIET

In the early morning hours
before the sun's quite up,
I wrap myself in still and quiet
and fill my empty cup.

ONLY IF I LET IT

I was up this morning
Before the sun even began to stir
When the sky was still full of stars
And the moon, bright

It was quiet

So very quiet

And I stood alone with myself
And my thoughts
While the cool of the air
Blushed my cheeks

Are you going to be alright?
I asked myself

Should be
I replied

Let me just stand here a little while longer and
breathe it all in
The cool, brisk air
With the scent of fall on the breeze
The starlight, the moonlight
And the idea that anything and everything is possible

And when the sun begins to rise?
I asked
Will the wonder of here and now disappear?

I thought about that
As I stood
Alone
In the dark shine
Of early morning
On the cusp of a day
Yet born

Only if I let it
I replied

DODDER

This river of life can be hard to navigate
Sometimes a joy...sometimes

I'm afraid to let go of the shore

Where is it taking me?
Where is it taking us?

The struggle to tread water
To stay in one place
And not drown
Is exhausting

But to let go...

Into the unknown...?

*

My dad loved to tell stories
of his sunlit golden days growing up in Ireland
rambling through the countryside
in the shadow of the Dublin Mountains

"Up from the Kimmage Crossroads," he'd say
is where he and the boys would run
Following the ambling River Dodder
away from prying eyes
to where they felt safe to set aside
their makeshift hook and string

And grow still

...becoming one with the river

"You had to go with the flow," he'd say,
"and let the water carry you away
Floating along with the reeds and weeds
to a place where the trout would hide"

And there

in that calm and gentle flow
armed with nothing more than a tickle
dinner was made

"Made in the shade," he'd say

But it was so much more than that

It was patience, trust, and understanding
And a reminder for now and for always...

to go with the flow

THE FALL

Black Pool
Deep and dark
I glanced it once
And nearly lost my way

Did you notice? Had you?

When I'd lost my breath
And turned away?

I resisted

...I resisted the pull
Of that dubh linn
As it sweetly tried to steal my heart
And on my mind, did prey

I wouldn't look
               "Don't look!" I cried
Digging my heels into shifting sands

               "Leave me not to betray!"

But...
It was just a look
Just one
And then

I fell

Softly
Gently

Longingly

Into the pitch and sway

*** dubh linn = dove lynn, which means black pool in
Irish***

BRAVE

I remember the day you died
You closed your eyes
after looking at me one last time
and went to sleep

Your breaths
long, soft, and slow

I held your hand
and looked at you
My person.
My perfect person.
Taking your final breaths
and me...
trying, helplessly, haplessly
to say goodbye
and thank you

And then it happened

There we stood
Hand in hand

at the edge of a great abyss
You were afraid to take that step
and I was afraid to let you go
to be alone in the world without you

But it had to be

I said, "I'll be okay"
Because I would

It was you, after all, who prepared me

Then, as always, you were brave

You took that step

And I knew
because of you
one day
I could be that brave too

On the day my mom passed I recall being in two places at once — the hospital room holding hands with my mom and an airy, ocean-like place where we stood holding hands. There was a kind of wall or new depth to the ocean that we couldn't see beyond. It was surreal. I told her I'd be okay and she could go, and she did.

ANAM ĊARA

Anam
  Anam
    Anam Ċara

Your light, it glows
and within it, I am safe
    enough to be silent
        ...revealing secrets I don't speak

This is my story.

And you love me, even still
As I love you

Across time
  The stars

    face to face

Your light, it guides me
it keeps me warm

And when I'm with you
Anam Ċara

I am
home

Anam Ċara translated from Gaelic means "Soul Friend."

An anam ċara can be anyone in your life who knows you inside out and loves you just the same (and you provide the same for them). Your love and friendship is not bound by time nor space.

THE PERFECT CUP OF TEA

When I was little, it was my Dad who would always put the kettle on. He swore that a good cup of tea could cure anything from nightmares to heartache, a scraped knee to the common cold, and everything in between. And if the tea wasn't strong enough — well, a hot toddy would do the trick.

He was right; a good cup of tea could cure almost anything — if he made it. And that, in itself, is the problem now. He's not around anymore, and I'm on my own to cure what ails me. I do make a good cup of tea, but it's never quite the same. One day, maybe I'll get the knack, but I'm not sure I want to. Not without him.

The true magic to my dad's cure-all cuppa came not from the tea, its time steeping in the pot, or just the right amount of milk added to the cup — that wasn't it at all — it was the man himself who held the magic. It was his care, his kind words, and his joking nature that could turn any problem, no matter how small or large, into no problem at all. That is, when he was in the right mood. He was an Irishman, who at times would go missing in his misery. I wish he didn't. I wish he could have stayed and never strayed into the recesses of his mind because when he was happy, the whole world seemed to sing in his chorus. It was in those moments that I wished time could stand still. He would stay that dad — happy, loving and full of magic — always. But he never did, and I think that may have made the tea even better...because it was fleeting.

I think about my dad just about every time I put the kettle on. Forever my father's daughter, chasing lost time and happy days in the perfect cup of tea.

LIFE

When I was little
I remember I couldn't wait for certain days to arrive
Christmas
My birthday
The last day of school...
And I recall my mother would say
"One day you'll wish it would all just slow down."
How she felt, the older she became, the faster time went...
My mind, being as it is, I tried to imagine that

Like matter, approaching a black hole
The closer it gets, the faster it goes
Life
Circling the black hole that is death
All of us wondering
But not knowing
If there is a light at the end
So we make up stories
To escape the fear
The pain
Isn't that what we're all doing?
Telling each other fairytales
In an attempt to banish the dark
And capture the light
Of all we do not
And cannot know
Until...

We do

THE LIFE STAGES OF A BUTTERFLY

Life happens in moments.
I was born. I graduated school. I bought
my first house. I married. I miscarried. My
marriage ended. My father died. My mother
was diagnosed with cancer.
I was diagnosed with cancer.

I was let go from my job.
My mother died.
The world as I knew it,
went black.

I felt like an angel of death. Like one of those
imposing statues you see marking someone's
grave: stoic, grey, lifeless.
Cracks forming across the surface of a once
alabaster exterior, no longer able to maintain a
flawless outward appearance.
Everything that I thought my life was; what
it was supposed to be; who I thought I was
supposed to be — gone in a moment.

I was a caterpillar.

Before the moments leading to my cancer
diagnosis and my mother's death,
I just was.
I walked along in the light, day by day.
Breathing in and breathing out. Not knowing
what it meant to live in the moment.
All of a sudden, it hit me.

I wanted to live.
I didn't merely want to observe life and dream
about what could be. That wasn't living. That
was watching television, watching the lives
of other people who may or may not have
been living in their moment. It was a strange
realization. Life and the prospect of it — what
I had missed by not living and what I might
miss because of my diagnosis — overwhelmed
me. And, I froze.

I cocooned.

I paced the floors of my house when I was
alone and cried in pain and torment.
The ground beneath me had fallen away.
I had cancer.
This was my life...

Cancer became a scary demon that I inwardly
battled. Outwardly I wore a smile and told
everyone that I was fine and that everything
was going to be okay.
I was not fine. *It* was not fine! And things were
not okay! They may never be *okay* again.
I don't know how I did it some days, but I kept
moving forward. One foot in front of the other.
Not knowing where I was going to end up.

My hair began to fall out.
My skin formed lesions that would not heal.

At night I would soak the bed with sweat, and I
would wake feeling like I'd been in a cold flood. I
would quietly get up and change the sheets. In the
morning I would be exhausted, and I would paint
on makeup, hoping to cover over the sores and my
tiredness. Then I'd arrive at work feeling successful.
Triumphant even! My mask was a good one today!
…only to be asked what was wrong with me?
I felt like a monster.
Digging down deep, I would find the extra
smile that I began carrying around in my purse, and
I would slap it on…all the while frantically searching
for a quiet bathroom, a closet, or any reason to go
back to my car — some quiet, safe space where I
could fall apart, if only for a moment.
Then I'd put that smile back on and try again. I
needed that job. Where would I be without it?

I cried out and clung on to whatever sense of
normalcy I could. Even when I knew it was wrong.
Illusion became the name of the game. Slap on a
façade, fantasize a little…spin helplessly out of
control like a whirling dervish. The wheels were
coming off at high speed, but I acted like everything
was fine.
People who called themselves my friends began to
abandon ship. In the light of day, the
true horrors of the mental side of cancer were too
much for some to comprehend. I could

barely blame them.
Still, it hurt.

Surgery and radiation slowed me down. I felt
like a human pin cushion from all the tests and
bloodwork. I felt nauseous and didn't want to eat
but still I would crave things I used to love, only to
eat it and not be able to taste it. And then get sick.

Some days I didn't want to leave bed. Other days I
couldn't. My body was heavy, my mind wishing it
could force time to rewind to a point where I could
change my diagnosis. Or to the future where I was
feeling myself again. I was living in every moment
except for the one I was presently in.

I lost weight and then gained it back from the meds
or…because my meds weren't right. What was it?
I waited for the doctors to let me know and for my
test results to start to become *normal*. I pondered
the idea of normal. What was that and when would
my *new* normal set in? I was in the future again,
hoping and waiting for the sick me to catch up.

Slowly, and not without great upheaval, things
began to get better. My medications started to
work and my moods, bloodwork, and energy
levels began to level off. My body was becoming
something I recognized again. Not some alien thing
that was not my own. My skin cleared, my weight
settled, my hair stopped falling out. I had colour in
my cheeks again, and I wanted to take part in the
world around me.

Sometimes the smile I wore was even my own.

I was transforming into a butterfly.
It was going to be worth it. I could feel it. The
struggle would not be for nothing.

Still. I was scared.
What if?
What if the cancer came back?
With every test and followup the wound
reopened.
What if? What if?...What if?
It was a beast that lingered around every
corner and in the shadows. Not just in the
shadows of my mind but everywhere I went.
Sometimes in the form of a movie, a magazine
article, a well-meaning friend...I even had
strangers declare, upon finding out that I'd had
cancer, that I should do any number of things
to prevent it from returning. Or, *Gasp!* That I
must have done any number of things to bring
it on.

I would pause to think...what if I had brought
it on myself? Would I not do anything and
everything to have it not return? "What if?"

"What if" I finally decided was a monster just
as dangerous as cancer.
I tried to ignore them both and did what felt
best for me.

As the days passed to weeks, months, and now
years…the monsters "What if?" and cancer
have faded but have not completely gone away.
I don't think they ever will. And, that's okay. I
don't fear them like I used to.

Once a caterpillar, now a butterfly.

I've survived.
I'm still here!
Alive in this moment.

STORYTELLING

Let me tell you a story
as my father would once tell me
of long ago and far away

It would come on the tail of twilight
coasting in
like the blanket
tucked up under my chin
in the soft, warm glow of candlelight

He'd tell tall tales of ghosts

And bulls left free to roam the fields
Of tickling trout
And orchard raids late at night

There were chocolates and oranges
and gates that would not
Could not
be closed...

And a dragon
who lost its might

because no one believed

I believe, I believe, I believe!

I'd call out

And I still do

In a whisper
to my father's ghost

in the quiet of the night

HOLD ON

To those who reach out, time and time again. Checking
in. Being the glue that holds things — some fragment,
haphazard as it may be, together.

I see you.

To those who hardly reach out at all
If ever
Always, "fine," not wanting to be a bother.

I see you, too.

I'm reaching back to hold your hand,
wipe your tears, and calm your quiet worries.

I'm reaching back.

Take my hand.

It's all going to be okay. Hold on.

❊

I hold you gently
in the palm of my hand.
You're so delicate and fragile.
Shaking through your tears,
you ask, "Why?"

over and over.
To which I reply,
"It's okay now.
You made it through."
"How do you know?" you ask.
And I say,

"Because I'm you."

LOOK FOR ME

Look for me

   I'm here

in the glint of your eyes
and the lilt of your laugh

Close your eyes
   there I am
where the lights glow
soft and warm

In the quiet moments
where your thoughts
   drift

And in your dreams
late
   late
     at night

Look for me

In those moments

when you think you're alone
and you take a deep breath

and wonder

"Where have you gone?"

I'm here
by your side
holding your hand
loving you as I always have
and will

forever more

SCARS

I have many scars
visible and invisible
and when I'm reminded
of one of them
maybe because I catch a glimpse
in the mirror
or a memory pokes at one
that's been quietly asleep for years
I think
I'm still here
I'm healing
and those scars are a symbol
of how far I've come

WE DON'T TALK ABOUT THAT

There's an old willow tree at the lake where my family used to have a cottage. At first glance, it's just a tree, a stately, beautiful, big old tree that has always been there. A part of the landscape and nothing more. I have never really looked at it beyond that. As I approached this time, I looked at it. I mean, I really looked at it, and it seemed alive in a way that made it more than just a tree. It appeared to move and contort into the shape of all of my female family members passed — my mother, grandmothers, aunts, riling and raging against the confines and deep grooves of the bark. The curves and knots formed their faces as they silently screamed for me to save them or hear them. Of course, I could do neither. Instead, I stood there looking on in a kind of awe and horror. As I did, one of the willow wisps caressed my cheek. I shuddered. It was just the breeze; I know it was. But I couldn't help but think that it had reached out and touched me.

Memories flashed in my mind, good and bad. Was it all just in my mind? I stepped away from the embrace of the tree to where the cottage itself now took centre stage. It lay there in ruin after the new owner decided not to do anything with it except sit on it, waiting for the property value to go up, then sell it again. It's been decades. A ramshackle vestige of a forgotten time representing the gilded age of post-war North America. It's a kind of prefabricated memorial to my family as they attempted to recreate a better life than what they had left behind in Ireland.

Our original family farm sits on the coast of the Atlantic Ocean. Hopefully, it wasn't as worn down as this place. It still belonged to me, though, in the years since the ownership had passed over, I had not gone to visit. I left the neighbour to care for it and to live with its ghosts. That's where it all started. Hundreds of years of my family's roots hanging their hats at the door. Here, on the shores of Lake Erie in Southern Ontario, a new generation tried to do it all over again, better and brighter. But they just made all the same mistakes. Now, here I stand; the current, and surely disappointing, culmination of it all. The last in my particular line.

I didn't know exactly what I was doing here, other than it sort of felt like home. I had arrived on this spot a few times over the years to feel grounded. The sound of the water lapping the shore usually worked to calm me down and bring me back. It wasn't working this time.

Between my miscarriage, my betrayals, my memories, and that tree — my mind wouldn't settle, and I couldn't catch my breath. My fingers grasped the new prescription of painkillers I had in my pocket. "Take one pill every 4 hours as needed," read the label. There was a week's worth of pills in there.

I was a mess. Everything that touched my life was a mess, and it occurred to me that I was the common denominator. If I wasn't around anymore, so many people would be set free. Especially me. Standing at the edge of the lake, I took a step forward. It was August, but the water was still a bit cool. Until that moment all I had heard were the thoughts inside my head.

Now, the soft hum of the breeze around me made itself known and I could hear it whisper through my hair and across my face, "Come home."

A chill went up my spine as I grabbed at the bottle of pills, trying to wrestle it open.

I paused and thought of my partner Patrick, waiting at home, wondering where I was.

Then, I heard movement in the water nearby. Tearing myself away from my own self-loathing, I looked up to see the dark figure of a woman looming toward me. A jolt of shock and panic filled my body. I turned to run and scream, but the sound caught in the back of my throat and my feet fumbled. I found myself face down in the stony sand of the beach. Quickly righting myself, I looked back, expecting the figure to be on top of me with my next breath. There was no one there. I raced for my car and within seconds was on the road, scanning my mirrors as I sped away. Where had she gone? Who was she? Had I imagined it all?

The scream that had caught in my throat earlier finally found its way out. It was the kind of scream that came from the whole of my body. The kind of scream that reached back across time to connect with me as a child, as those long withering fingers of the family friend made their way up my shorts; to the thirty-something me as I found out that my husband was having an affair; to the slightly older me as she lost her father and then her mother; to the untethered me as she was told that she had cancer and who then lost her job when she told her boss; to the me that felt lost and alone and vulnerable, grasping for anything that might take away the pain; and finally, to the me who had just lost another baby. Together, crammed in my car, we screamed so loud that I thought the windows might shatter. Then, one by one, we fell silent, disappearing into the night leaving the present me alone in my car, speeding along the lonely stretch of highway.

"Come home." the whisper called again.

(From a fictional work in progress)

BLOOD

Admit it
   After all these years
you wish
   I had never been born

If only you could

You were hurt
   I know that
and you're hurting
   I know that too

an old wound reopening
every time you look at me
or hear my name

I'm a reminder
the one who remains...

a living, breathing someone

to blame

WHOLE BUNCHES AND WHOLE BATCHES

How I long to go home again. The daylight sun fades softly into the night sky and the moon and stars begin to shine.

My thoughts wander to when I was a child.

It seems so long ago…

I travel back across time and the ocean, far away to a little Irish town on the coast of the Irish Sea. There, the waves beat a soft rhythm that slowly lulls me to sleep. I was just small, only seven or so, fighting my heavy eyes, thinking of all the things I might miss.

Downstairs, my family gathered around the kitchen table, telling stories, laughing, and singing songs while the whole of the small town came knocking down the door wanting to take part in the festivities.

Before bed, I sat perched on my grandmother's lap. "She has to be part fairy," she said because of my blonde hair, fair skin, and light eyes. My grandmother loved to fill my head with stories and warnings meant to protect me from the "little people" who must have wanted to carry me away. "Don't go standing in fairy circles or go wandering into the woods alone. Certainly, don't go into the sea without your father, or else the selkies might try to steal you!" She would tickle my nose and it seemed a game but at the same time serious. So, I avoided the fairy rings, and I dared not wander into the woods on my own, even though they seemed inviting.

But the sea. I couldn't help but paddle my feet in the water whenever I had the chance. "Oh no. Now, pet!" my granny would call out. "Get her away from there. She's gone in far enough!" My dad would come in after me, but instead of bringing me back, he would take me further out for a swim. My granny and mom were left in a panic at the shore, but I knew I was safe and so had no fear. I dared the selkies to come for me. If only to see one up close.

It was magic — all of it. How could I possibly go to bed at the end of every wonderful day? And, so I fought, as only a small child could.

"A glass of water, please?"

"Just half an hour more?"

"Another story, Granny, another cuddle?" *More, more, more!*

Peeking through the rail at the top of the stairs, I listened to the happy voices from below. I watched their shadows dance along the floor and up the wall to where I sat, mesmerized. Eventually, though, I was caught and ushered back to bed where, at some point, I would give in and sleep would take me away. My dreams filled with fairytales.

One night as the bedtime ritual began, my dad presented me with a question. How did I want to be taken up to bed? Did I want to be carried like a baby, like a sack of potatoes, like an airplane, or did I simply want to hold his hand?

"Whatever way you choose," he said, "I will tell you a story, and then you must promise to go to sleep."

I thought over my choices as my mother helped me brush my teeth and climb into my pyjamas.

"Like a baby," I said when I met him again in the kitchen and before saying my goodnights.

"Aww, a little baby," my sisters teased, pinching my cheek and tossing my hair.

"Now, now," Dad said, "like a baby it is." And he whisked me up into his arms, and the story began...

*

"Once upon a time," Dad said, as one does when they tell a story to a child. "Far, far away, there lived a little girl who was the baby of the family, just like you. She was a lucky little girl. In fact, her birthday was all sevens. She had parents and a family who loved her, a house with a room in it all her own. And anything she wanted she could pretty well have. There aren't many children around the world who can say that," Dad said, and I agreed.

"When I was a little boy, I was the baby like you. But..." his voice trailed off as he looked around my room, "I had to share a room with my brothers, and my dad wasn't often home. When he was, I wasn't sure that he loved us. But my brothers and I found magic and happiness where we could, just the same. You see, even when things don't seem very good, if you try, you can find happiness and beauty. You just need to look." My dad wiped a tear from his eye. "We didn't have money for toys like you have, but we had fun anyways. Fishing, running through the fields and mountains, and eating apples when the trees in the orchard were ripe. Can you imagine that? An apple was a treat for me and my brothers. And oranges and chocolate!" he exclaimed. "I didn't eat an orange or have chocolate until I was about five — not much younger than you are now."

I gasped. We always had oranges and apples and chocolate in the house.

"You see, how very lucky we both are?" Dad said as he lay me down in bed and tucked the covers up under my arms. "Now imagine, as you fall asleep, what life would be like if you had never had an orange. Imagine that you'd never ever eaten chocolate and you had no room to call your own. And..." he paused, "you had no mom or dad to tuck you in at night. How different your life would be? How the simplest of things, like this orange, could be so — beautiful." He placed an orange in my hands and kissed my forehead goodnight. I stared at the orange, and I felt a bit sad. "Always remember," my dad said before he shut off the light and went back downstairs, "that you are my baby, and I love you whole bunches and whole batches. I will always keep you safe and you will always have everything you need and most of what you want. Just remember, not every child is as lucky as you."

The light from the moon was just bright enough that I could still make out the orange in my hands. I smoothed over its dimpled skin with my fingers. I thought of all the lovely things I had and how lucky I was. I didn't think to get back out of bed, and I didn't think of all I might be missing downstairs.

The next morning, I ate that orange for breakfast, and it was the best orange I had ever had. My mom cut it up with apples and cooked them with a touch of cinnamon and brown sugar. Then she presented them to me on a fresh-baked scone topped with butter and shavings of chocolate. I never looked at oranges or apples or chocolate the same way again.

❈

When nighttime came around the next night, my dad once again asked how I wanted to be carried up to bed. This time, though, being carried like a baby wasn't an option. I could be carried over his shoulder like a sack of potatoes, like an airplane, or I could walk holding his hand.

I chose to go as a sack of potatoes. And what fun that was!

Dad hoisted me up over his shoulder, and my head and arms dangled behind his back. I giggled and laughed all the way up the stairs and into bed where he once again tucked me in. This time, instead of an orange, he presented me with a potato. I made a face, to which my father laughed. "Ah now, to an Irish child many, many years ago, that potato would have been just as remarkable as that orange I gave you last night!"

I was hooked and the story began…

"Once upon a time, long ago and not so far away, there lived a child your age who had never seen an orange. He hadn't even heard of one. But a potato! Now that was something. A good, big hearty potato could keep him feeling full all day."

"Just a potato?" I asked.

"Just a potato. With maybe a sneaky little pad of butter on it if he were very lucky." I stared at the potato, even more mesmerized with it than I had been with the orange the night before. I couldn't imagine eating just a potato and being thankful for it.

I thought about the day I'd just had and of all the wonderful things I'd eaten: my breakfast, lunch — the dinner! Not to mention the cookies and cakes, and many other treats too.

"When your great-grandfather was a little boy, the potato was all that he and many other little boys and girls had to eat here in Ireland. One day, they all went rotten in the ground."

"Then what did they do?" I asked.

"For many of them, there wasn't anything they could do," Dad said plainly, and I struggled to know what that meant. "Those little boys and girls and their mams and dads went hungry. Some of them died. Others had to move far, far away and some, like your great-grandfather, learned how to live without the potato. You see," Dad continued," there were no grocery stores back then like there are now. If you didn't grow your own food or hunt for it, you simply would not eat. Can you imagine that?"

I could not.

"Close your eyes and imagine with me." And so I did. "The fields are black with rot, everywhere. All you could do was hope that if you had animals like chickens and cows, they would stay healthy enough to keep providing eggs and milk. But if you were starving, they would be too. Off into the forest you would have to go, or down by the seaside, hunting and foraging for food.

Banding together with his neighbours, your great-grandfather and his family were able to survive. But they had to be careful. The authorities were not nice and if they found you with food, they might just take it away for themselves. Everything was done in secret, especially at night, under the cover of the moon. It was a dangerous and sad time here in Ireland."

My dad kissed my forehead and told me how he loved me whole bunches and whole batches. He shut the light off and I lay there, holding onto the potato. I listened to the waves outside as they lapped against the shore. I imagined men, women, little girls, and boys sneaking out to take a curragh (a boat) out to sea in hopes of quietly catching some fish to eat in secret. Maybe they would gather some other things along the way that they could eat and share with others. Yet, here I lay holding tight to one potato. One of many more stored in the kitchen downstairs. I hugged that potato and thought about all of those who weren't as lucky as me, and I never looked at a potato the same way again.

The next day, we had fried potatoes with our breakfast, french fries with lunch, and colcannon with dinner. I watched my granny make the colcannon over the aga, where a hot fire burned inside. All the smells hit my nose, and my tummy began to rumble. First, my granny peeled and boiled the potatoes and cabbage with a bit of salt. Then, in a heavy pot, she seared some thick-cut bacon. The potatoes and cabbage were strained and mashed with lots of butter, and then the bacon was mixed in with green onion and salt and pepper to taste. She held a spoon out for me to try. I smiled, trying again to imagine life without potatoes. Granny placed the whole pot into the oven to keep warm while she, my mom, and my aunts finished making the rest of the dinner. There was fish and beef and lamb — the table was filled with delights and with people busily passing plates, bowls, and trays this way and that! For me, the best was still the colcannon, and I enjoyed every bite and even asked for more.

❉

It was bedtime once more and my options for going to bed were only two — like an airplane or holding my dad's hand. I chose to be carried like an airplane.

Sweeping me up into his arms, my dad placed me face down with one arm wrapped tight just above my knees and the other secured just under my arms. My instructions were to keep my arms outstretched and my legs straight. "Close your eyes now," Dad said, "and imagine that you're flying up above the clouds. The land below is falling away, making all the buildings and people almost too small to see. Imagine that among all those people are your family and you wave goodbye to them, not knowing if you will ever see them again. Soon, all you can make out is the patchwork of green that is Ireland and, in the distance, the ocean. And, beyond the ocean, you don't know." My dad set me down on my bed.

"Is that the whole story?" I asked. "That seems very sad, to fly away and maybe never see your family again."

"It does seem sad, doesn't it?" Dad said matter of factly. "But that's my story. And you know, of course, that I did get to see my family again. For a little while, though, I wasn't sure. You see, when I was barely a grown man — I had just turned eighteen — I decided that my best future lay in Canada. Ireland was in hard times and if I were going to make my mark on the world, I decided that I had to leave."

"Was it hard to go? Were you afraid?" I couldn't imagine leaving and travelling far away from home. The thought of never seeing my parents again was almost too much. I could feel tears forming in the corners of my eyes.

"It was very hard, and I cried many nights on my own, calling home once or twice just to hear a familiar voice or two." My dad wiped away a tear or two of his own. "But I had to do it. Imagine if I hadn't? I wouldn't have found my way to you, to your sisters, or to your mom…" My father trailed off in thought for a moment. "I had to be brave. We all must do that at some point. Be brave and take a chance." He said, "We need to spread our wings and fly, taking all that our parents have taught us and go off into the world and live the best life we can. Your great-grandparents did it, your grandparents… me and your mom. Each generation tries to make things better for the next. One day it will be your turn." My dad smiled. "What will your story be?"

What *would* my story be?

That's what my father left me with that night. A thought. Just a thought and, as always, he said, "I love you whole bunches and whole batches." Those two things together made me feel strong. I was loved, and I was free to choose my own story.

I thought of how brave and strong my dad had been venturing so far away from home all alone. I thought of my granny and how she must have worried. I wondered, "Could I be so brave and strong one day, if I had to be?"

When I woke the next morning, no one else was up. I gathered jam, bread, and butter to the table and set each place with a cup for tea, a small plate for bread, a napkin, and a spoon for stirring. When my granny and parents arrived on the scene, they marvelled at what a good job I had done and how very grownup I was. I smiled, and when we were all done with breakfast I helped tidy up.

It was a new day and new adventures were waiting.

❖

That next night I didn't wait for my dad to find me for bed. I stood beside his chair at the kitchen table and held out my hand. "Right, then," he said with a smile. "You realize that tonight, it's you who will tell the story?"

I did, and I was ready.

Taking my dad's hand in mine, we began our journey.

"Once upon a time, in the future." I looked up at my father with a cheeky grin, thinking I was very clever. "There lives a young girl who is almost all grown up. She decided when she was still small that she would grow up to make herself and her parents and their parents very proud. She would do that by sharing stories with children about how hard things used to be a long time ago, and how they still are for some. The girl would grow to become strong and brave. She would fly across the ocean and not be afraid because she knew that, back home, her parents would be waiting for her. She wouldn't need her dad to carry her to bed or to hold her hand anymore." I sat down on my bed and placed my legs under the covers and lay down while my dad tucked the blankets in around me to finish the job.

"I hope," he said, looking a little bit sad, "that even though the girl doesn't need to hold her dad's hand anymore that she will still want to, from time to time."

"Of course!" I said.

And I did.

Growing up, there were many times when there was nothing better than to see my dad's arm outstretched with his hand waiting there for me to hold.

As long as my dad's hand was there — I felt invincible.

But one day, my dad's hand was gone.

That's when I learned his final lesson.

Love.

To have love and to give love.

Whole bunches and whole batches.

~The End~

*Whole bunches and whole batches is something I remember saying, (and being said to me in return) when I was small in response to "I love you."

I'm not sure how it started or why, but it's a happy memory I have of my parents and family and one I treasure. And so I share it.

To the Moon and Back
The Story of the Mother Deer

***a story based on folktales of old.
Dedicated to my mom.

Many moons ago when nature still ruled the world, the winter solstice had arrived.

It would be the longest night of the year.

The last night that the moon would reign over the sky before giving way to the sun.

Before the sun could once again shine, the sun goddess Danu had to return. It was the task of Breya, the Mother Deer, to guide her home.

Breya had a fawn named Freya who would join her on her journey.

And what a journey it was!

Freya followed her mother through darkness into light.

They trudged through snow, forests, rivers, and streams — meeting many friends along the way.

But not everyone they met was friendly...

The sly wolf wished the night would never end, and every year she would set traps, tell long stories, barter, and even lie all to try and slow or stop Breya's journey.

In the end, Breya and Freya would always take to the sky and return with the sun.

"To the moon and back!" Breya would say to her young fawn. For, just beyond the moon, in the winter's sky, lived the sun. Resting and awaiting another year when it would take over from the moon.

This year, Freya was ready and waiting for her mother to begin their journey. However, something was different.

Something was wrong.

Freya couldn't find her mother in any of the usual places.

She stopped to inquire with the wise old owl, the mother and father rabbit and, finally, reluctantly...the wolf.

Approaching the wolf's den, Freya could see that the door was open.

Inside was a fire, and sitting in its glow — her mother's golden antlers.

"I seem to have won our little game this year," said the wolf, slyly, from the entrance of her den.

"Not if I can help it!" said Freya pushing past the wolf and soaring off in the direction of the moon.

Freya, remembering everything her mother taught her, made her way confidently through the night sky.

She danced among the quiet snowflakes that fell softly to the ground below.

She flew straight through thick storm clouds, and when she reached the moon, she paused. She was almost there. Rounding the moon, Freya saw it. The warm, glorious light of the sun. Freya stopped, not knowing what to do next. How could she bring the sun home without her mother?

Her antlers weren't large enough, and she wasn't as wise or as strong!?

"To the moon and back," Danu said appearing with Breya by her side. The two, goddess and deer, became one.

Danu showed the fawn her reflection.

And it was then that Freya realized she was now Mother Deer. All of those years spent following her mother had taught her all she needed to know.

"It's your turn now." said Danu.

Harnessing the sun between her golden antlers, just as her mother before, Freya carried its light home. The Winter Solstice was over for another year.

Upon her return, the wolf greeted Freya with a nod. She wasn't a bad wolf...she was...well...a wolf. It was her nature.

Like all the other animals in the forest, she knew that the sun would always return, despite her tricks.

It was the way of the world. A world in which there was a plan — where one cycle ended and another began.

"Even the darkest, longest night," paused the wolf, "will always awaken into sunlight."

Freya was now the bearer of the light every Winter Solstice.

Soon, her own fawn, Fianna, would join her.

Together, mother and daughter would fly to the moon and back until one day it would be Fianna's turn to learn that she too was a goddess and that within her lay the strength to harness the sun and make it shine.

The beginning...

HOPE

With every moment that passes
Every phase of the moon
Sunrise and sunset
There is hope

Look for it
Feel it
Breathe it in

Give it time

UNBROKEN

Sometimes
You might think
That life
Is trying to break you
That it's taking you away from who
You think you're supposed to be

Hold on

One day
You might find yourself looking back
Thinking
I made it
I'm still here
Unbroken

And

While you might not be exactly who you were at the start
Somehow
You're even more of who you were always
Meant to be

AT THE TABLE

I feel a bit like me again. You know?

I went away for a while, a long while...a few
years, actually.
Though I never really left.

It was my mind, maybe my soul? Whatever
it was, it went away. It took a backseat to
the unravelling world around me. It sought
solitude and fantasy. A place where nothing
ever changed, and everything always stayed
the same.

I lost myself.
I died with those who died close to me. I died a
little more when I thought, "What if I die?"

The world around me changed, and I couldn't
keep up.

People left. Don't they always?
Who could I rely on when the one I relied on
most had gone away?
It wasn't their fault. But who was I now, that
they were no longer home?

I drowned in the new world I found myself in.

Alone.

I can't say that I fought my way back because
how could I? I didn't know who I was. I didn't
know where I was going. I just kept moving.
Forward, in whatever direction opened to me.
Feeling things out. Was the water warm, or
uninviting?
Slowly, I could feel a change.

I was waking up.

Nothing is the same and nothing ever will be
but I think I'll stay anyways.

There's a place set for me.

CHANGE

Change comes to everyone
and it comes to teach us
what exactly might not be immediately clear.
Be patient.
In time, and if you're open to it, you will come

to understand.
Remember this...
What is meant for you will find its way.
There is hope in that.

EMPATHY

Without a second thought
We so casually turn a blind eye
To the struggles of others

The medicine we all need...
The cure that could save us all...
Empathy

*

How I wish that some of the things that
happened to me hadn't...
If I could rid myself of that pain
and the memories...
But I can't
That's not how life works
Pain will come and pain will go
I had to ride the waves of life in my way
Trying to remember that when I was floating along
Others were drowning
and my empathy
is what could help keep them afloat

SEE YOU AGAIN

I scan between the seconds that tick by
I can see you there
Smiling

I try to hold you there for as long as I can
Before you slip and fade away
I'll see you again

ON READING

I wanted to run
But I couldn't
So I dove into a book
Devouring every word
Soaring over every page
Becoming fully immersed
If not completely lost
in the story
It wasn't mine
But for a while I would pretend that it was

And for a while
I was free to run
Madly in love with my escape

GASLIGHT

Even a gaslight can expose the truth given enough time.
What if...it wasn't Eve that took the first bite?

THE APPLE

There was an apple
It was lush
and ripe
I reached for it
But before I could grasp it
he took it
and ate it
a piece lodging
in his throat
forever
A reminder of his sin

he told everyone
I did it

That it was

All

My

Fault

*My mother once told me that I was going to be blamed for things I didn't do. And, that no matter how I might try to say I hadn't done those things, I would never be believed. I asked what should I do? And she said, "If it's something you want, you might as well do it."

WONDER

Have you ever looked out
upon dewy grass
on an early summer morning?

Freshly crusted snow
beach sand
rippling waves
or even asphalt
under the light of the sun
or full moon?

Do you recall that sparkle?
That sense of magic and wonder you felt at the
sight of
that shimmering light
that no matter how you tried
you couldn't catch

to hold in your hand
and keep forever
just the same

Some people are like that

Leave them alone
Let them shine

THE LITTLE THINGS

All the little things
It seems
Are what I remember
What I miss the most
The simple things
Gestures and
Thoughts
A knowing look
A laugh brought on by a memory
That only we shared

To have you in my corner
To know that you were there
I miss that
Most of all
And when I think about it all again
They're not little at all
In fact, they're quite big

All the little things
Really aren't little at all

NONSENSE UNREFINED

I sit
I sat
I sought
Meaning to words
Clambering in my mind
And when meaning didn't come
I thought myself
Rather dumb
But that was truly unfair
Because it was just

Nonsense

Unrefined

DAD

Just for a minute
I let my feet slide into your shoes
They were big
and clunky
and I knew I wouldn't be able to walk in them
But I could imagine what it was like
to wear them all the time

And it was hard

FIND A WAY

That dis
ease
You feel
From that which you
Don't
Won't
or feel you
Cannot
Express...
Will eventually turn
into
Disease
Of the mind
The body
The soul...
Of one

Of all

So, find a way

TONIC AND GIN

My mind seldom rests
And at times I wonder

Why
Why can't I sometimes just do
Nothing at all
And then I remember
for a woman
To do nothing
Would be a sin
Then I laugh the good laugh
Thumbing my nose
Sipping slowly, my tonic
and gin

THE INVISIBLE WOMAN

I sense something happening to me
Something not right
Yet, I feel if I tell you, you'll not see it
Replying that
I'm wrong
And there's nothing to worry about

It's the kind of something that's happened time and time
again throughout the centuries

To someone like me
A woman
Whose words are taken
After all they couldn't possibly be my own

And I'm made
Voiceless

Rendered
Invisible
Gone

SILENCE

There's so much I want to talk to you about sometimes...
so I do. I talk to you like you're right here with me.
And it feels like old times...and then I stop talking, half
expecting, half hoping, that you'll reply. But you don't.
There's only silence, and it hurts so much.

MAD

They're mad because I won't be who they want me to be
I'm not who they thought I was
Can you tell me how it is
that I haven't yet gone mad?

SNAPSHOT

I might not have everything, but sometimes I really feel
like I do. There's a magic in the moment sometimes...
those I'm with, the feeling in the air, the warmth of it
all and the love...and I try to soak it all in. Like taking
a snapshot in my mind that I'll be able to carry with me
forever.

You Can

Some very bad things happened

Not all at once
But bit by bit
And they began to break me
First my heart
And then my mind
Until...there I was
In pieces all around
On the ground
Crying
Calling out for something
Someone
No longer there
I gasped for air
Knowing deep down
That I was alone
How could I go on?
"I can't!" I cried
And yet something deep down inside replied
"You can."
It was a whisper through my veins
That sounded so familiar

It was you
You'd never left me

WITH LOVE

With Love

I fell apart
And after a while
I carefully began to pick up
my broken pieces
Saying,
"I love you"
To each and every one

And that...

That's how I
put myself
back together again

STARDUST

You're stardust
A spec of light
Edging your way
Through the universe
Small though you may be
You are growing
Consuming the darkness
Surrounding you
Enlightening the world
Around you
And nurturing the fire
Within

There's another world waiting for us
Beneath the surface of this one
In places where nature thrives
And pavement dies

WINTER

There's a stillness in winter
a silence
that comes from the gentle falling snow
It calls us to listen
to the beat of our own hearts
and to the ancient wisdom
of our ancestors
whispering through our veins

MAGIC

Sometimes when I close my eyes I can imagine
things just as they used to be

The sights

The smells
The feeling

And for a moment...

It's magic

HEART FALLS

Soft as snow
My heart falls
More deeply in love
With you
Everyday

MY OWN

What is my name?
Is it the one assigned?
The one HE gave me

Or the one I choose for myself?

Should it matter?

What's in a name...?

Hers
His
Mine or ours??

It will take some thought
In the end I will choose

MY GRANDMOTHER

Inside a jumbled mind
decades have come and gone
yet live in the now

and then

only God knows when

the film slips through the projector's grips

and clicks
staring out through darkened eyes
wrinkling at the crease, they twinkle
while thinned lips, upturn
singing a song long since sung
and whose words aren't quite right

♫ I'll be seeing you again
In all the old familiar places

Some sunny day ♫

And,
for but a moment

They remember

OLD STORIES

Remember who you are
The words whispered softly

I didn't
At first
But I learned

Samhain
Sow-in

Remember the stories
Your ancestors
And light the fire
Outside
Then, within

Speak your stories
Refresh your memory
They're there in
Your bones

A Recipe for Healing

You ask
Sometimes loud
Other times quiet
Much of the time
Unspoken

And you wonder why no one hears you?

Because...
We're all crying out
Looking for help
To heal the pain

When we understand that we're all hurting
Empathy grows
And healing begins

I Wish You'd Ask

I was crazy to think that someday we might
understand each other
when you don't seem to understand yourself

We are all broken
Every single one of us
From one generation
To the next
Until
Someone not only wonders
But asks

And keeps asking

Why?

Glass

I used to think I was made of brick
Solid and sturdy

Why? Because my parents told me so

And then
I started losing things
People
Ideas
Myself

I was translucent
And cracked

With a few chips here and there

I was glass

I tried to hide
I wanted to hide
But it was too late
Others saw me
And saw through me
And they began to throw stones
Wondering when I might break
Forgetting that I was human too
Just like them
And that we're all made of glass
We might pretend we're other things
But we're not

And when I realized that
When I was almost nothing more
Than sand
I looked at myself again

I was still made of glass
But I was also something more
I was light

Refracted
Inward and outward

Vulnerable, yes
But also
I was hope

RUGBY

As in rugby and in life...sometimes you have to
go backward to move forward.

I LET YOU GO

I let you go

the idea of you
the "what could have been"
but wasn't
and never would be
except in my thoughts
and restless dreams

The heartbreak

of giving up

  the struggle

and pushing against the waves
of expectation
only to find myself
caught in the calm
of the riptide
pulling me out to sea
and the great unknown

I let go
away with the current
away with the flow

Two Row

There is a

space
                between

you and I
but it doesn't need to
divide us

What if
we found again
the common ground;

Two Rows
living side by side

Paddling down the river
'neath the old growth trees
let us all give pause
and listen...

Our collective
heartbeat
growing stronger

Louder!

calling out to your children:

Come Home

OUR HOME ON NATIVE LAND

The time has come
For the sun to set
On your empire
No more honour or glory
Only a legacy of horrors
And unmarked graves
The lives of innocents
Violated, murdered
Hidden away
Assimilated and erased
...you hoped
While the rest of us
Stood blindly and idly by

Eating your soup
And taking of your sacrament
Believing every word
Of your lies...
Happy and Glorious
Glorious and Free

No more!
Do we stand on guard
For thee

NEVER FORGET

Something in me shut down
the day you died

Time stood still
and in some ways
I'm still there
even though I moved on

My mind trying to forget
what my body never will

The shock, the knowing,
the *trying to keep it together*

I don't want to remember
what I'll never forget

I'M EVERYWHERE

It's interesting
how your eyes move across me
as if I'm not even there

While inside your mind...

my existence is everywhere

MANITOULIN

Take a breath
Take it in
Close your eyes
And listen

Hear the water ripple and flow
While it slowly, rhythmically, laps the shore

Feel the breeze kiss your cheek
And the sunlight warm your soul

This is where time stands still
Where warblers and chickadees meet the
morning light
It's where a lone loon sings its haunting lullaby
in the peaceful calm of night

This is the place where the fire crackles and
burns
It's where your spirit comes alive in the glow of
the embers as they touch the sky;
Dancing with fireflies
Learning to live among the stars

This is where you remember who you are
And why you're here

So, try it again
Like you mean it this time

Take a breath
Take it in
Close your eyes

And listen

MAKE BELIEVE

I made a photo of you in my mind
It goes with the story I made up
From the scraps you left behind
You're not real
Not my version...

But if it's okay I'll steal
Away sometimes
And find you in the dark
Imagining what never could

Possibly might have
Maybe

Been

THE BROKEN

We are not born broken
but how quickly we become
Inheriting the brokenness of our parents
then developing our own
cracks and breaks

No, we are not born broken
but we are
born to break

Some will shatter into a million tiny pieces
worn by the wind
into a fine sand
scattering like dust
A memory fading with time
and with it the reasons why
And so
the same mistakes resurrect

But still
there are others
who though they may break and shatter
will not become dust

They rebuild
one jagged broken piece

at a time
Limping upward and forward
into the light

Just as we are born whole
meant to break
to shatter

We are also born resilient

Never knowing if we are destined for dust
or a mosaic

At least
not until the moment arrives

When we truly break

BACK TO YOU

What if
Is a dangerous game we play
And the funny thing is it always brings me back to
You

THE WILD INSIDE

I didn't let the wild in

   It was already there

      I only had to let it out

It had been locked up in the dark
Many moons ago
Before I was born
Before my parents were born
And theirs too
   And so on
      And so on

Until one day
I felt it

The wild inside

Its ivy trellised out from my lungs
And wrapped around my heart
Scratching and crying to be set free

My mother wasn't sure...
and my father said I should think about it so
that I would be

So I did

And I kept it in
And thought
   And thought

And thought
    About the wild inside

I tried to make sense of it

I really did

Did it fit here?
Or did it fit there?

But it didn't seem to fit in anywhere

Almost
But not quite

The wild inside;
One day, like an ancient, old bear, humbled by its days
in the sun
And the next, a young new rabbit, learning and
growing as it ever reached for the moon

I couldn't keep it locked up
The wild inside

It wasn't fair

But I was afraid

Ashamed

What if no one liked it?
The wild inside me?

Then I grew and the rabbit and bear grew with me
and I could see that the wild...

Was everywhere

Uncertain and untamed

I smiled to know I wasn't alone
and slowly
Opened the door

Wild

  and free

BEAUTIFUL HEARTBREAK

That's life.

We are born
And play in the sun
All the while watching
The shadow of night
Slowly set in
Losing who we hold dear

We carry on though
One step at a time
Seeking out the sunrise
Of each new day

Until it's time for our sun to set

Make sure
as much as you can
that it goes down
in a blaze of colour...

And beautiful heartbreak

OLD GROWTH AND FORGOTTEN STORIES: THE CAILLEACH

I met an old woman by the river the other day, and had I been in proper possession of my senses, I would have been afraid. But I wasn't, even though she had only one eye, jagged teeth, and skin that was as craggy as the dolostone rocks that jut up from the forest floor.

Yes, had it not been for the happenings of the previous two days...I would have been afraid.

About a week ago, we, my husband and I, moved to this place where our home backs onto hundreds of acres of protected forest, rivers, streams, and small inland lakes. Being surrounded by so much solitude and nature is what we have always dreamed about when thinking of where our future home should be. And this place is steeped in beauty and history and a kind of magic that I couldn't quite put my finger on. But I wanted to. I wanted to be connected to this place, to honour it, and to have it feel like home.

As if I belonged.

It's been so long since I've felt like I truly belonged anywhere.

The first week in our new home was spent setting up the house and making it, well, a home. With that done, or at least well on its way, it was time to explore more fully the world beyond my backdoor. So, off I went, GPS in hand, water, cellphone, you name it, I had it as I trekked deep into the forest until I came upon these trees — the largest trees I'd ever seen. Towering high above every other tree nearby. They were like the grandparents of the forest. I was, and ever will be, in awe of them. They remind me of just how small I am. These trees must be hundreds if not thousands of years old. I counted seven of them sitting council over the rest of the forest.

Powerfully rooted in their place, these trees were both connected and knowing. I wonder, and I hope that one day I might feel the same.

A raven called out from one of the branches high above, and I stood watching it watch me. This went on for a few minutes until it flew away. I followed it and as I turned, I swallowed my breath with a heavy gulp and froze. A herd of white-tailed deer stood semi-circle around me. For the life of me, I don't know how I didn't hear them approach. Slowly, one of the female deer stepped closer, and I instinctively reached out a hand as she extended her nose to smell it. Then, out of nowhere came a loud crack from somewhere even deeper inside the forest. It sounded like a large branch or maybe a whole tree crashing down. Not surprisingly, the noise startled the deer, who rushed and leapt over me, the sound of their stampede quickly fading into the dark unknown expanse of the woods. I lay on my back looking up, my heart about to beat from my chest. What must the large old growth trees be thinking of me? And I'm not sure if it was a sign, but I began to laugh. Were they laughing at me too? At me and not with me? The idea of me as a silly woman, naïve in the ways of nature, flashed through my mind.

I decided that was enough for one day, and I set off for home. All the while, feeling like I wasn't alone.

The next day, late in the morning, I ventured to the same spot in the forest — the somewhat clearing by the river amongst the council of old growth trees. Today, I packed a lunch and some apples in case I should meet the deer again. But they did not come, and after sitting for a while enjoying the scenery and birdsong, I placed the apples around the base of one of the trees — the one I deemed to be the oldest and largest. "For our friends, the deer," I said. Just as I finished setting the last apple down, I heard the raven call out. I looked up just in time to see it fly away from high above the spot where I was standing.

Then, everything went quiet and still. The leaves stopped rustling, the birds stopped singing, and the hair on the back of my neck stood on end.

Turning slowly, I expected to find that the deer had returned.

They had not.

Instead, I found a large black wolf standing only a few feet away. I froze, but unlike the day before with the deer, I did not extend my hand. I may have been a silly woman, but I wasn't that silly.

We stood, the wolf and I, staring at each other for what had to have been only minutes. However, when I finally blinked, the sky was growing dark, and the wolf was gone. I searched all around expecting it to reappear at any moment. When it didn't and when it was obvious to me that it was gone, I gathered up my things and swiftly and observantly started for home. My husband met me on the path not far from the house.

"I thought I'd lost you," he said. "I've been home about an hour and when you didn't return in that time, I thought I'd better get out looking before the light was totally gone for the night. What happened?"

"I lost track of time out there." I said, "That's all. I'm fine. I'm sorry to have worried you." We hugged and as we ate dinner, I told him what happened.

"You're not going out there again tomorrow, I hope?" he asked.

"I have to," I replied. "It's strange...I'm afraid but I don't feel like I'm in any actual danger, if that makes sense."

"It doesn't," he said. "Just promise me you'll be careful."

"I promise."

That night, I dreamt of the raven, the deer, the wolf, and those beautiful old growth trees. What did it all mean? And, when I woke the next morning, I could hardly wait to get out into the forest again. So, as soon as my husband set off for work, so did I.

This is when I came upon the old woman, not being the least bit surprised. As with the two previous days, she appeared after the raven had made its call and flown away. And after all, had grown quiet. In fact, when I first saw her, I thought she was just a rock. A large dolostone rock, of which there are many. But something told me this wasn't just a rock. So, I closed my eyes and looked again.

And there she was.

"Aye," she said. "Your eyes are not playing tricks on you. I'm as real as real can be. Do you know who I am?" she asked, searching my face for some sense of recognition that didn't come. Her smile fell and was replaced by disappointment. "Ah, well," she said. "I'm not sure why I would think you would remember. No one ever does. But I always hope just the same."

"Who are you?" I managed to ask. It's not often an old woman turns into a rock or a rock becomes an old woman. I didn't know what to believe. "Should I know you?" I asked further.

"You should," she said. "Like the rest, you've forgotten. A real shame and all." The old woman stared off into the distance.

"How so?" I asked, following her gaze down river then up to the top of the ancient, old growth trees.

"This forest used to be full of trees like these," she said. "I've visited here many a time over the years as I followed your lot, hoping you'd let me stay with you. But you didn't. All of you, pale-skinned and searching, some of you running..." she trailed off. "In any event, like them, you're looking to start over. And in doing so, you forget."

"Forget what?" I wanted so badly to understand.

"Who you are and where you've come from." The old woman's gaze narrowed in on me. "Do you know why you're here?"

I felt confused. "I...I...," I stumbled. "I wanted to go for a walk to feel connected."

"Ah ha!" she declared. "To feel connected to nature." Her smile had returned.

"Yes," I said.

"But this is not your land," she said simply.

"No, it's not...," I looked down and scuffed the ground with my shoe.

"Look up." The old woman demanded. And I did as I was asked. "Where are the rest of them?" She motioned up to the old growth trees.

"I don't know," I said.

"But you should," she demanded. "Maybe it wasn't you who cut them down, but you should at least acknowledge that others like you did."

We stood in silence.

"The land does not forget." The old woman continued. "You might forget but the land does not."

"I'm sorry," I said, unsure of what else to say or do.

"Don't apologize to me," she said. "Apologize to the trees, the land, the waters, and the people who have called this place home, long before you came calling." The ground beneath us began to tremble. "If you want this place to be your home, you must...remember."

"How do I remember something I've never known?" I asked in earnest.

"Ah, but you do know. Deep inside, you do," said the old woman. "Like the trees are connected to the earth and rock and everything in between, so are you."

"How?" I asked.

"Through story," she said.

"I don't understand."

"That's clear...there is much too much misunderstanding. I'll ask you plain and clear: What are the old stories of your people in the land from whence you came?"

"I don't know?" I replied.

"That's the difference between you and the people of this land. They still have their stories. They know who they are," the old woman said. "Try as some of you have over the years to take their stories, their language, their children, and their ways from them...you haven't been able to. But you did manage to lose your own." She threw her hands up to the trees.

"How do I find them again? My stories, I mean?"

"Go back. Find the old storytellers and books and reclaim them. Don't go around taking from others what isn't yours to be had," said the old woman. "Your stories and history have much to teach you."

"And when I learn them, then what?" I asked.

"You'll have, I sincerely hope, a new understanding of yourself and the rest of the world." The old woman smiled, looking again to the top of the trees. "We're all connected."

"Will you at least tell me your name?" I turned but all I found was a rock, cold and grey. Atop it sat the raven and, in its mouth, a leaf from one of the old growth trees. The raven looked at me, cocking its head from side to side before letting go of the leaf and flying away. I watched the leaf float gently to my feet before picking it up and smoothing it out across the palm of my hand. And as I did, the veins within it came to life. They moved and contorted themselves to spell out a name, that repeated on the wind...

"Cailleach."

BE YOURSELF

Being positive is great. But, as the saying goes, sometimes too much of a good thing can be bad.

Telling someone who is feeling anxious or scared or uncertain to just be positive and that everything will be okay or that it could be worse can seem insensitive and invalidating to that person.

Let them be who they are and be true to how they feel. These are normal emotions — ones that we all face at some point or another.

What to do instead — listen. Try to understand. Think back to a time when you were feeling anxious or scared or uncertain. Or be honest with yourself. Maybe you're feeling those things too. If you are, that's okay. ♥ It's normal.

What isn't normal is faking how you feel or doing so because others say you should.

Be yourself. Your feelings are valid and so are those of others.

MY MOM

There's an old photograph of my mother in a box of mementos from a time gone by. A time before I was born when my mother was a woman and not just my *mom.* There she sits, living a life all her own, full of dreams and possibilities. She faces the camera, a sly Mona Lisa smile effortlessly gracing her face. Behind her, a bustling town comes to a halt.

It's a moment frozen in time. A freeze-frame on a life I knew little about. I wish I knew more. To know my mother when she was young and carefree as if that were even possible — was it? She must have been once upon a time. She certainly looked the part as I linger over the photograph that lies like glass in my hand. Whether she was or wasn't, I will remember her that way. No longer captive of a life that she often wanted to escape but never did.

To have been able to sit down with her, just two friends having a laugh over a glass of wine. What secrets might she tell me that I didn't know as her daughter? What life and loves filled her days before I was even a glimmer in her eye?

She was a real, live woman. Just like me.

Imagine that?

THE WILLOW TREE

There have been a few times when I thought I might break. I thought for sure I was going to. When my mom passed, it felt like the very last of what I could manage. It was as if the floor was falling away from beneath me, and I was going to be swallowed whole. Part of me hoped for that. A place where time could stand still. Even just for a little while, so I could catch my breath. But, life doesn't work that way.

In the face of great adversity, it's essential to give yourself time and permission to grieve, collect your thoughts, process, and live in that moment, no matter how uncomfortable it may feel. Running from it doesn't make it better — it simply buys a bit of time before it returns, ready to be dealt with.

There's no time limit on grief. No limit on figuring out who you are and where you're going.

The world can wait. In fact, it will bend with you as you sit in your silence and slowly make your way forward.

There are still days when I wonder how it is that I have arrived where I am. My steps forward after my experiences with loss, grief, and cancer were, at many points, messy to say the least. Yet, here I am.

There's a willow tree on the site of a place my family used to gather. I visit it at least once a year. It sits at the very edge of a lake known for rough storms. It has survived all of them over its many years. Bending in the storm...but never breaking.

LET IT OUT

"How are you?" you ask.

My mind races

There's nothing worse than having a thousand
things to say. Every word and thought
scrambling for first place in my mind,
only
to catch
in a lump
at the back of my throat...

unsaid

"I'm fine," I reply.
"No really?" you press on.

"There's so much I want to say but I can't make
sense of it. Not yet."

"That's frustrating."

"It is," I say, "but I think if I scream...it might
help."

So I do
And I'm not alone
You're screaming too

We're all screaming

At the top of our lungs

YESTERDAY'S GROUND

The path set by yesterday's ground is gone
And that of tomorrow is uncertain
All that is certain is that which is under your feet
Now
One step, in front of the other

Standing still is an option, but that does not mean
that the world around you will stand with you
Because it won't

Though the walls may fall away
And all the people leave
And change
The home fire will still burn
Bright in your heart
And in your mind's eye
'Til the time comes
For its light to guide you home
And you'll know it at once
For all who gather
will greet you
And know you
By name

SIT WITH ME

Sit with me...
even though we're far apart.
Just close your eyes and think of me.
Hold this space,
across the miles
and feel the warmth of
a thousand smiles.
Sit with me...
and we'll make it through.
You and me
and me and you.

LOOK FOR ME

Look for me

  I'm here

in the glint of your eyes
and the lilt of your laugh

Close your eyes
  there I am
where the lights glow
soft and warm

In the quiet moments
where your thoughts
  drift

And in your dreams
late
  late
    at night

Look for me

In those moments
when you think you're alone
and you take a deep breath

and wonder

"Where have you gone?"

I'm here
by your side
holding your hand
loving you as I always have
and will

forever more

*

I look for you in dreams
   Among the stars
and shimmering embrace
   of the moon

I look for you and
= I hope
   Because...
     if I didn't
      my heart

would break

GATHER THE STARS AND HANG THE MOON

Walk with me
where the wild wind blows
Where orchids bloom
and hollyhocks grow
For home we are
And none too soon
So gather the stars
and hang the moon

Made in the USA
Las Vegas, NV
17 November 2023

81019112R00083